GW01019095

Gallery Books
Editor: Peter Fallon

SELECTED AND
NEW POEMS

Eamon Grennan

SELECTED AND NEW POEMS

Gallery Books

Selected and New Poems
is first published
simultaneously in paperback
and in a clothbound edition
on 17 August 2000.

The Gallery Press
Loughcrew
Oldcastle
County Meath
Ireland

ISBN 1 85235 275 2 (*paperback*)
    1 85235 276 0 (*clothbound*)

The Gallery Press acknowledges the financial assistance
of An Chomhairle Ealaíon / The Arts Council, Ireland,
and the Arts Council of Northern Ireland.

Contents

for Rachel, Kira,
Conor and Kate

Wherever you are, you touch the bark of trees
testing its roughness different yet familiar.
— Czeslaw Milosz, 'Throughout Our Lands'

Facts of Life, Ballymoney

I would like to let things be:

the rain comes down on the roof,
the small birds come to the feeder,
the waves come slowly up the strand.

Three sounds to measure
my hour here at the window:
the slow swish of the sea,
the squeak of hungry birds,
the quick ticking of rain.

Then of course there are the trees —
bare for the most part.
The grass wide open to the rain,
clouds accumulating over the sea,
the water rising and falling and rising,
herring-gulls bobbing on the water.

They are killing cuttlefish out there,
one at a time without fuss.
With a brisk little shake of the head
they rinse their lethal beaks.

Rain-swollen, the small stream
twists between slippery rocks.
That's all there's to it, spilling
its own sound onto the sand.

In one breath, one wink, all this
melts to an element in my blood.
And still it's possible to go on
simply living
as if nothing had happened.

Nothing has happened:
rain inching down the window,
me looking out at the rain.

Swifts over Dublin

Stop, look up, and welcome these
artful dodgers, high-flyers on the wing,
these ecstatic swirlers, sons of air
and daring, daughters of the slow burn,
who twist and kiss and veer, high
as kites on homecoming. Survivors,

they've put their night-sweats by,
harrowing darkness in a rumour of wings
and companionable squeaking, riding the blast.
And now, how they celebrate a comeback, casting
high-pitched benedictions down
on shopping centres, stray dogs, monoxide traffic.

From any point of view
they are beyond me, dark sparks of mystery
I must look up to, where they usher
the full flush of summer in, highly
delighted with themselves and sporting
their keen, seasonal dominion.

In the National Gallery, London

for Derek Mahon

These Dutchmen are in certain touch
with the world we walk on. Velvet
and solid as summer, their chestnut cows
repeat cloud contours, lie of the land.

Everything gathers the light in its fashion:
that boat's ribbed bulging, the ripple
of red tweed at the oarsman's shoulder,
the way wood displaces water, how water
sheens still, the colour of pale irises.

See how your eye enters this avenue
of tall, green-tufted, spinal trees:
you tense to the knuckled ruts, nod
to the blunted huntsman and his dog,
a farmer tying vines, that discreet couple
caught in conversation at a barn's brown angle.
You enter the fellowship of laundered light.

From the ritual conducted around this table
these men in black stare coolly back at you,
their business, a wine contract, done with.
And on brightly polished ice, these villagers

are bound to one another by the bleak
intimacies of winter light — a surface
laid open like a book, where they flock
festive and desperate as birds of passage
between seasons, knowing that enclosing sky
like the back of their hands, at home
in the cold, making no bones of it.

On a 3¹/₂ oz Lesser Yellowlegs,
Departed Boston August 28,
Shot Martinique September 3

for Phoebe Palmer

Little brother, would I could
make it so far, the whole globe
curling to the quick of your wing.

You leave our minds lagging
with no word for this gallant
fly-by-night, blind flight.

But ah, the shot: you clot
in a cloud of feathers, drop
dead in a nest of text-books.

Now seasons migrate without you
flying south. At the gunman's door
the sea-grapes plump and darken.

A Gentle Art

for my mother

I've been learning how to light a fire
again, after thirty years. Begin (she'd say)
with a bed of yesterday's newspapers —
disasters, weddings, births and deaths,
all that everyday black and white of
history is first to go up in smoke. The sticks
crosswise, holding in their dry heads
memories of detonating blossom, leaf. Saved
from the ashes of last night's fire,
arrange the cinders among the sticks.
Crown them with coal nuggets, handling
such antiquity as behooves it,
for out of this darkness, light.
Look, it's a cold but comely thing
I've put together as my mother showed me,
down to sweeping the fireplace clean. Lit,
you must cover from view, let it concentrate —
some things being better done in secret.
Pretend another interest, but never
let it slip your mind: know its breathing,
its gulps and little gasps, its silence
and satisfied whispers, its lapping air.
At a certain moment you may be sure (she'd say)
it's caught. Then simply leave it be:
it's on its own now, leading its mysterious
hungry life, becoming more itself by the minute,
like a child grown up, growing strange.

Something After All

Sitting in what was my father's
and is now my mother's house, I wonder
will the mirror tell me what I have become.
Beyond the back window
the valedictory arms of the apple tree
wave the last of their vivid spirits
at the white drift of gulls going down
from the mountains to the sea. Sunlight
makes the vulnerable colours of the neighbourhood
hall-doors shine. The other is the sunny
side of the street this morning, and I sit
in shadow, imagining a Chinese poet
who sees this world through half-closed eyes
and sees nothing but apple blossom
brushing the stalks of his hair, the stem
of his neck, and senses
beyond question, this is it.
Two sparrows light in the rose-bush
that claws across the garden wall:
they nibble its maroon-green leaves.
In the garden behind this widowed house
the wild broom is a holy show, menacing
the mild air with extravagant dazzle,
while last month's daffodils have given up
their lemon-headed ghosts and settle
back in their natal earth again, knowing,
I suppose, exactly who they are.
And are at home, reposed as one
who believes in the bright life of blossom,
fruit, and falling leaf — at home
in the ineffable air of his own country
between the mountains and the sea. *It is*,
he says to himself or dreams he says,
how it is. The day endures in his breath,
in the light pooling his eyes; shadows live

like cats in the back garden, and the doors
on the sunny side of the street are shining,
if I can believe my eyes, like new leaves.

Mother and Child

for Joan

You form a warm nest for him
where he creeps in each morning
I'm away. Content, he curls up
near your heat, and you slip
head-first into sleep again,
knowing well what you've made flesh
of your flesh, of your bone, bone.

You drift between dreams.
You see his red hair shining
over the book he has propped
upright against the mound of hip
and stretch of thigh. Early light
finds your dark head on the pillow,
whitens the bony wing of his arm.

All day I've carried it around
like an old photograph:
the vaulted warmth of your body lifting
and letting gently fall the bedclothes,
light beginning to bloom in his hair.
How his grave eyes slide across the page
slowly, like loving hands.

Winter

Who, when they are all gone,
will you be to yourself? You swallow air
like ether edged with razor-blades,
run squeaking over frozen snow.

Summer was like love and marriage:
you could scarcely see the cold
coming through a haze of fat grass,
flesh. You wake and find it's done for.

This weather brings us to our senses:
pity the fox, the melancholy badger,
the fieldmouse clean as a snowflake,
shivering and praying in the flayed hedges.

Muse, Maybe

You are never at home with her.
Private, she shies the familiar touch.
Lady of half-lights,
you cannot make her out from shadows.
There's no catching up with her:
she sleeps near your sleep;
your mind wears her face like a mask.
She's the lady of changes.

She's the girl you kissed in the graveyard,
hers the warm skin under a raincoat.
You turned sixteen that winter, speechless
at heart, for all your speeches.

She wears the air of what's possible,
making your pulse ache. *Find me out*,
she says, *put me in the clear*.
You've made such promises before.

Lying Low

The dead rabbit's
raspberry belly
gapes like a mouth.

Bees and gilded flies
make the pulpy flesh
hum and squirm:

O love, they sing
in their nail-file voices,
we are becoming one another.

His head intact, tranquil,
as if he's dreaming
the mesmerised love of strangers

who inhabit the red tent
of his ribs, the radiant
open house of his heart.

Night Driving in the Desert

Move fluent as water
splashing brightness. Imagine
jackal, badger, wild goat,
fox-eyes glinting like broken glass:
gingerly they sniff the sour exhaust.

Remember greenness; name
its distant children: *ryegrass,
olive, avocado, fig* —
first sweetness welling in the mouth.

Herbs the Arabs call *ashab*
sprout inside a single rain,
rush to blossom fruit seed,
staining the sand with rainbows.

Imagine a procession of tanager dresses
drifting through plaited shadow:
women crossing the earth like water,
sunlight splashing their skin to stars.

I know it is over in a flash
and after
my heart is beating wildly, wildly for days.

For the Record

After six unsparing days of storm
a grey still day without rain.
Nothing spectacular, no exploding
stars off the lake, no precious
glitter of soaked grass, no triumph
in bannering branches, just branches
taking the air as if it belonged
to them, the faint sleepy *chink-*
chink of the robin in the next field,
and everything back in its place.
But nothing carnival or sabbatical,
only a steady domestic peace
secures all animations in the garden,
giving everything its due. No fuss,
no unexpected flares, no amazing
grace in the play and swift trans-
figurings of light off water. Only
cloud, seamless still air, this hush.
So, after six days of storm, record
a perfectly ordinary day at last —
dry, a little on the cool side.

Incident

for Louis Asekoff

Mid-October, Massachusetts. We drive
through the livid innards of a beast — dragon
or salamander — whose home is fire. The hills
a witch's quilt of goldrust, flushed cinnamon,
wine fever, hectic lemon. After dark,
while water ruffles, salted, in a big pot, we four
gather towards the woodfire, exchanging
lazy sentences, waiting dinner. Sunk
in the supermarket cardboard box,
the four lobsters tip and coolly stroke each other
with rockblue baton legs and tentative
antennae, their breath a wet clicking, the undulant
slow shift of their plated bodies
like the doped drift of patients
in the padded ward. Eyes like squished berries
out on stalks. It's the end of the line
for them, yet faintly in that close-companioned air
they smell the sea, a shadow-haunted hole to hide in
till all this blows over.
                          When it's time,
we turn the music up to nerve us
to it, then take them one by one and drop
in the salty roil and scald, then clamp
the big lid back. Grasping the shapely fantail,
I plunge mine in headfirst and feel
before I can detach myself the flat slap
of a jackknifed back, glimpse for an instant
before I put the lid on it
the rigid backward bow-bend of the whole body
as the brain explodes and lidless eyes
sear white. We two are bound in silence
till the pot-lid planks back and music
floods again, like a tide.

                              Minutes later,
the four of us bend to brittle pink intricate
shells, drawing white sweet flesh
with our fingers, sewing our shroud-talk
tight about us. Later, near moonless midnight,
when I scrape the leafbright broken remains
into the garbage can outside, that last
knowing spasm eels up my arm again
and off, like a flash, across the rueful stars.

Wing Road

Amazing, how the young man who empties
our dustbin ascends the truck as it moves
away from him, rises up like an angel
in a china-blue check shirt and lilac
woollen cap, dirty work-gloves, rowanberry
red bandanna flapping at his throat. He plants
one foot above the mudguard, locks
his left hand to a steel bar
stemming from the dumper's loud mouth
and is borne away, light as a cat, right leg
dangling, the dazzled air snatching at that black-
bearded face. He breaks to a smile, leans wide
and takes the morning to his puffed chest,
right arm stretched far out, a chequered china-blue wing
gliding between blurred earth
and heaven, a messenger under the locust trees
that stand in silent panic at his passage. But
his mission is not among the trees: he
has flanked the sunlit rims of Wing Road
with empty dustbins, each lying on its side,
its battered lid fallen beside it, each
letting noonlight scour its emptiness
to shining. Carried off in a sudden cloud
of diesel smoke, a woeful crying out
of brakes and gears, a roaring of monstrous
mechanical appetite, he has left this unlikely
radiance straggled behind him, where the crows,
covening in branches, will flash and haggle.

Traveller

He's ten, travelling alone for the first time —
by bus to the city. He settles an empty seat
and waves out at where I stand on the footpath
waiting for him to be taken, barely a shadow
grinning behind smoked glass. To his eyes
I'm a dim figure far off, smiling and waving
in a sea of traffic. Behind me, the blinding sun
melts down the black back of hills
across the Hudson. For all there is to say
we are deaf to one another
and despatch our love in shrugs and pantomime
until he gives thumbs-up and the bus
sighs shut, shuddering away from me. He mouths
words I can't understand; I smile back
regardless, blowing a kiss through the air
that starts to stretch and empty between us. Alone,
he stares out a while, admiring his height
and speed, then reads two chapters of *The Dark
is Rising*. When the real dark leaches in
he sees nothing but the huge loom
of a hill, the trees' hooded bulk and
come-hithering shadow. He tries to curl up
in sleep, but sleep won't come, so he presses
one cheek flat against the cold black glass
and peers past his own faint ghost
up at the sky, as any night-time traveller
would — as Henry Hudson must have, sailing
his *Half Moon* past Poughkeepsie, already
smelling the Pacific. My son seeks the stars
he knows: Orion's belt, his sword, his dog
fall into place, make sense of the dark
above his voyaging. *When I found him*, he says,
I felt at home, and fell asleep. I imagine
him asleep in his rocky seat there,
like that wet sea-boy dozing at mast-head,

whose lullaby the whole Atlantic hums
in the lull between storms, the brief
peace between battles, no land in sight.

Father in Front of a Picture

Vermeer's girl leans her sleeping head
on the neat curve of a wristbone, her propped
elbow taking the weight. Warm
fleshlight and lived-in familial shade
share the open doorway and watch over her
like a father, I imagine, while she snatches
brief sleep, dreams he'll be
standing in her light when she wakes.

This agate-keen December day — a few
green streaks of grass breaking the bleak
amnesia of snow; nuthatches, finches,
chickadees quick as spring in the famished
branches — I must imagine how
my own two children will grow
to know my absence
like a hint of pipe tobacco fading
as you enter a familiar room, like a light
on the landing gone out before
you've quite dropped into sleep, and you lie
alone in the dark and know the dark
disputed borders of yourself, your self,
for the first time. How their sleep-warm

skin shivered when I came home
cold from my early-morning walks
this time of year, nuzzling them awake
with my rimey beard and the names of birds
I'd seen — a frost-edge glitter of wingtip
and tailfeather springing to startled life in that
drowsy room. No knowing whether they'll ever
remember such mornings, now we're separate,
or know only my absence
like warm light bulging an open doorway

while they wish themselves to sleep, to dream
me there watching them all night until they wake
and with their own eyes find me, large as life.

Jewel Box

Your jewel box of white balsa strips
and bleached green Czechoslovakian rushes
stands open where you keep it shelved
in the bathroom. Morning and evening
I see you comb its seawrack tangle of shell,
stone, wood, glass, metal, bone, seed
for the bracelet, earring, necklace, brooch
or ring you need.
                              Here's brass from Nepal,
a bangle of African ivory and chased silver
for your wrist, a twist of polished
sandalwood seeds, their deep scarlet
gleaming like the fossil tears
of some long-gone exotic bird
with ruby crest, sapphire claws. Adriatic
blue, this lapis lazuli disc will brighten
the pale of your throat, and on this small
alabaster seal-ring the phantom of light
inscribes a woman tilting an amphora, clear
as day, almost as old as Alexander. To the
ebony velvet brim of your hat you'll pin
a perfect oval of abalone, a dark-whorled
underwater sheen to lead us to work
this foggy February morning. We'll leave
your nest of brightness in the bathroom
between the mirror and the laundry-basket
where my dirty shirts sprawl like
drunks amongst your skirts and blouses. Lace-
work frills and rainbow silk pastels, your panties
foam over the plastic brim, and on the shower-rail
your beige and talc-white bras dangle by one strap
like the skinned Wicklow rabbits I remember
hanging from hooks outside the victuallers'
big windows.

We've been domesticated strangely,
love, according to our lights: when you
walk by me now, naked and not quite dry
from the shower, I flatten my two hands
on your wet flank, and wonder at the tall
column of flesh you are, catching the faint
morning light that polishes you pale as
alabaster. You're warm, and stay a moment
still like that, as though we were two planets
pausing in their separate orbits, pendant,
on the point of crossing. For one pulse-stroke
they take stock of their bodies
before returning to the journey. Dressed,
you select a string of chipped amber
to hang round your neck, a pair of star-shaped
earrings, a simple ring of jet-black,
lustrous onyx. So, going down the stairs
and out to the fogbound street, you light my way.

All Souls' Morning

Rain splatting wet leaves; citrine light; the cat
scratching the sofa; the house dead quiet
but for the furnace thumping in the cellar; that man,
my neighbour, out on Locust Road as he is each morning,
whatever the weather, walking his dog. Bent shoulders,
heavy head, a cherry leash dangling
from a pale hand, his dog the dark tan of oakleaves
when they turn and hang and enter the depths
of winter. I see a huge patience in his stoop, in that
ghostly cigarette limp between his lips, the stiff
tilt of his head, the treadle action of his passage,
the orange surprise of a golf umbrella blossoming
from one fist, the loll of the dog by his side as they
return up Locust, eager to be in again from the cold
wet day that's breaking round them. I'm thinking how,
bound to one another, they've been at this
for years, when my father comes leaning as he always did
up Clareville Road, not far from where he's buried, bent
against the bitter wind that tunnelled it in winter,
his black umbrella furled, our small black
terrier, Brandy, straining the leash towards home
where my mother fusses the tea together. Five o'clock
and Dublin's dark already, being November. Fat raindrops
scud the wind and mix with his lost thoughts
as he hastens after his dog and home to the wife
who, when he leaves her behind, will run aground with grief
at being no one in the world. This is the bottom line:
we button our habits to the chin, then set out, any weather,
walking with death. Here I hear a bluejay's screech
rattle the skeleton of our locust tree. The road beyond
my window is empty again and rain gives way
to skybright weather: grey aquarium light
makes luminous the air, coating dark tarmac
with mirrorpools of periwinkle blue. The rising wind
tides among survivor leaves, and a swallow-flock of dead ones

joyrides Locust Road, cold no more, borne off. *All night,*
you said when we wakened warm by one another,
I was seeing shapes widen round the room, hearing them
whisper in the wall. And now my hungry children come
clattering to the kitchen for breakfast. The house quickens.

Soul Music: The Derry Air

A strong drink, hundred-year-old
schnapps, to be sipped at, invading
the secret places that lie in wait and
lonely between bone and muscle,
or counting the seconds round the heart
when it stutters to itself. Or to be
taken in at the eyes in small doses,
phrase by somatic phrase, a line
of laundry after dawn, air clean as
vodka, snow all over, the laundry
lightly shaking itself from
frigid sleep. Shirts, flowered sheets,
pyjamas, empty trousers, empty
socks — risen as at a last day's dawn
to pure body, light as air. Whiteness
whiter than snow, blueness bluer than
new day brightening the sky-lid
behind trees stripped of their illusions
down to a webbed geometry
subtler than speech. A fierce blue eye
farther off than God, witnessing
house-boxes huddled together
for comfort, that blindly front
the deserted streets down which in time
come farting lorries full of soldiers.
You are a fugitive *I*, a singing
nerve; you flit from garden to garden
in your fit of silence, bits of you
flaking off in steam and sizzling
like hot fat in the snow. Listen
to the pickers and stealers, the shots,
man-shouts, women wailing, the cry of kids
who clutch stuffed dolls or teddy bears
and shiver, gripping tight as a kite
whatever hand is offered. Here

is the light glinting on top-boots, on the
barrel of an M-16 that grins, holding its
hidden breath, beyond argument. And here
is a small room where robust winter sunlight
rummages much of the day when the day
is cloudless, making some ordinary potted plants
flower to your surprise again, again,
and again: pink, anemic red, wax-white
their resurrection petals. Like hearts
drawn by children, like oiled arrowheads,
their unquestioning green leaves seem
alive with expectation.

A Closer Look

for Peter Fallon

Simply that I'm sick of our wars and
the way we live, wasting everything we touch
with our hands, lips, tongues, crowding
the earth with early graves, blind
to the bright little nipples of rain
that simmer on willow twigs, amber shoots
of the stumped willow itself a burning bush
on the scalloped hem of the ice-pond. So
I'm turning to winter beasts instead, their
delicate razor's-edge economies as they
shift for themselves between dens, migrant
homebodies like the souls we used to have,
leaving behind them in the shallow snow
their signatures, the thing itself, illiterate
signs that say no more than *We were here*
and mean it: handprints, footprints, midnight-
mahogany blossoms of shit, citrus and
mustard-green swirls of piss that brighten
the eye-numbing, one blank world. Porcupine,
possum, raccoon, skunk, fox — behold them
combing the cold land for a bite, not just
taking for granted their world as it comes
and goes. They wear the weather like a shawl,
following their noses through a sphere of
sudden death and instant satisfactions. They lie
in the sunlit pit of sleep, or the worm of hunger
unwinds his luminous tail to rouse
and send them coldly forth, sniffing the wind
the way lovers browse word by word by word
first letters for what stays salted
and aromatic between the lines. It isn't
innocence I find in them, but a fathoming
depth of attention anchored in the heart, its

whorl of blood and muscle beating round — the way
they traffic between frosted starlight
and the gleamy orbs of berries and last apples,
between storm in the big cloud-bearing boughs
and the narrow breath of earthworm and beetle
barely stirring the dead leaves, now all
quivering dash, nerves purring, now the wildfire
flash of pain that lays them, an open secret,
low. I try to make my hopeless own of this,
to sense in myself their calm unthreading
between brisk teeth or busy mycelian fingers,
breaking — as we will — down to our
common ground, the whole story starting over
in the old language: air first, then
ooze, then the solid lie of things, then fire,
a further twist, begin again. Making do.

Men Roofing

for Seamus Heaney

Bright burnished day, they are laying fresh roof down
on Chicago Hall. Tight cylinders of tarred felt-paper
lean against one another on the cracked black shingles
that shroud those undulant ridges. Two squat drums
of tar-mix catch the light. A fat canister of gas
gleams between a heap of old tyres and a paunchy
plastic sack, beer-bottle green. A TV dish-antenna
stands propped to one side, a harvest moon, cocked
to passing satellites and steadfast stars. Gutters
overflow with starlings — lit wings and whistling throats
going like crazy. A plume of blue smoke feathers up
from a pitch-black cauldron, making the air fragrant
and medicinal, as my childhood's was, with tar. Overhead,
against the gentian sky, a sudden first flock whirls
of amber leaves and saffron, quick as breath, fine
as origami birds. Watching from a window opposite,
I see a man in a string vest glance up at these
exalted leaves, kneel to roll a roll of tar-felt flat; another
tilts a drum of tar-mix, till a slow bolt of black silk
oozes, spreads. One points a silver hose and conjures
from its nozzle a fretted trembling orange lick
of fire. The fourth one dips to the wrist in the green sack
and scatters two brimming fistfuls of granite grit:
broadcast, the bright grain dazzles on black. They pause,
straighten, study one another: a segment done. I can see
the way the red-bearded one in the string vest grins and
slowly whets his two stained palms along his jeans; I see
the one who cast the grit walk to the roof-edge, look over,
then, with a little lilt of the head, spit contemplatively
down. What a sight between earth and air they are, drenched
in sweat and sunlight, relaxed masters for a moment
of all our elements. Here is my image, given, of the world
at peace: men roofing, taking pains to keep the weather

out, simmering in ripe Indian-summer light, winter
on their deadline minds. Briefly they stand balanced
between our common ground and nobody's sky, then move
again to their appointed tasks and stations, as if they were
amazing strangers, come to visit for a brief spell
our familiar, shifty climate of blown leaves, birdspin. Odorous,
their lazuli column of smoke loops up from the dark
heart of their mystery; and they ply, they intercede.

At Home in Winter

1

We sit across from one another
in front of the fire, the big logs
clicking and hissing. Outside
is bitter chill: locust branches
grow brittle as crystal. You
are sewing a skirt, your pursed mouth
full of pins, head spinning with
Greek and Latin. You frown
so not to swallow any pins
when you try to smile at me
slumped under the *TLS* and bewailing
the seepage of my days, the way
my life runs off like water, yet
inexplicably happy at this moment
balanced between us like a tongue of flame
skiving a pine log and seeming
to breathe, its whole involuntary life
spent giving comfort. It would
be a way to live: nothing
going to waste; such fullness
taking off; warm space; a fragrance.
Now the sight of you
bending to baste the blue skirt
before you pleat and sew the waistband in
enters and opens inside me, so
for a second or two I am an empty centre,
nothing at all,
then back to this home truth
unchanged: you patiently taking
one thing at a time as I can't,
all the while your head beating
with hexameters and foreign habits. I go on
reading in silence, as if I hadn't

been startled into another life
for a fiery instant, inhaling the faintly
resinated air that circulates
like blood between our two bodies.

2

Blown in from the noonwhite bite of snow,
I find the whole house fragrant as a haycock
with the soup you've stirred up, its spirit
seeping into closets, curtains, bedrooms —
a prosperous mix of chicken stock, carrots,
garlic, onion, thyme. All morning
you've wreathed your head in it, and now
you turn to me like a minor deity of earth
and plenty, hands dipped to the wrist
in the flesh of vegetables, your fingers
trailing threads from the mound of bones
glistening on the counter-top. You stand
at the edge of a still life — glazed
twists of onion skin, papery garlic sacs,
bright carrot stumps, grass-green delicate
stems of parsley, that little midden
of bones — and I behold
how in the middle of my daily life
a sober snow-bound house
can turn to spirit of chicken, air
a vegetable soul, and breathe on me. Turning
back to the stove, wooden spoon
still steaming, you say
in no time now we'll sit and eat.

Four Deer

Four deer lift up their lovely heads to me
in the dusk of the golf course I plod across
towards home. They're browsing the wet grass
the snow has left and — statued — stare at me
in deep silence, and I see what light there is
gather to glossy pools in their eight mild
barely curious but wary eyes. When one at a time
they bend again to feed, I can hear
the crisp moist crunch of the surviving grass
between their teeth, imagine the slow lick of a tongue
over whickering lips. They've come
from the unlit corners of their fright
to find a fresh season, this early gift, and stand
almost easy at the edge of white snow islands
and lap the grey-green, sweet
depleted grass. About them hangs an air
of such domestic sense, the comfortable hush
of folk at home with one another, a familiar something I sense
in spite of the great gulf of strangeness
we must look over at each other. Tails flicker
white in thickening dusk, and I feel their relief
at the touch of cold snow underfoot
while their faces nuzzle grass — as if, like birds,
they'd crossed unspeakable vacant wastes
with nothing but hunger shaping their brains, driving
them from leaf to dry leaf, sour strips of bark,
under a thunder of guns
and into the cold comfort of early dark. I've seen
their straight despairing lines cloven in snowfields
under storm, an Indian file of famished natives, poor
unprayed-for wanderers through blinding chill,
seasoned castaways in search of home ports,
which they've found at last, here
on winter's verge between our houses
and their trees. All of a sudden

I've come too close: moving as one mind
they spring in silent waves
over the grass, then crack snow with sharp hard snaps,
lightfooting it into the sanctuary of a pine grove
where they stand looking back at me — a deer-shaped
family of shadows
against the darker arch of trees
and this rusting dusk. When silence settles over us again
and they bow down to browse, the sound of grass
being lipped, bitten, meets me across the space
between us. Close enough for comfort, they see we keep
instinctively our distance — knowing our place, sharing this air
where a few last shards of daylight
still glitter in little meltpools
or spread a skin of brightness
on the ice, the ice stiffening towards midnight
under the clean magnesium burn of a first star.

Morning: the Twenty-second of March

for Rachel

All the green things in the house
on fire with greenness. The trees
in the garden take their naked ease
like *Demoiselles d'Avignon*. We came awake
to the spider-plant's crisp shadow
printing the pillowcase
between us. Limp fingers of steam
curl auspiciously from the cup
of tea I've brought you, and a blue-jay
screeches blue murder beyond the door.
In a painting over the bed
five tea-coloured cows stand
hock-deep in water at the broad
bend of a stream — small smoothback stones
turtling its near margin. A brace
of leafy branches lean over it
from the far bank, where the sun
spreads an open field like butter,
and the cows bend down
to the dumbfound smudge of their own faces
in the flat, metallic water. And here
this minute, at the bristle tip
of the Scots pine, a cardinal
starts singing: seven compound metal notes
equal in beat, then silence, then
again the identical seven. Between
the sighs the cars and pick-ups make,
relenting for the curve with a little
gasp of gears, we hear over the road
among the faintly flesh-pink
limbs and glow of the apple orchard
a solitary dove throating three sweet
mournful *Om*, then falling silent, then —

our life together hesitating in this gap
of silence, slipping from us and becoming
nothing we know in the swirl that has
no past, no future, nothing
but the pure pulse-shroud of light, the dread
here-now — reporting thrice again
its own silence. The cup of tea
still steams between your hands
like some warm offering or other
to the nameless radiant vacancy at the window,
this stillness in which we go on happening.

from *Conjunctions*

I'm in the dark, going home fast
along the Palisades, the night roaring and flashing
with the cars I pass, that pass me, all our lives at hazard
on the simple spin of a wheel, locked anonymously into
this meteor shower above the legal speed limit. I have
been handing over to Joan the children, as happens
every other week-end: we meet at a gas-station and
deliver our children up — lovingly, to take the sting
out of it — to one another. I'm thinking about this,
about the way my words can't catch it yet but
about must, and about must go — trying to be true
to the unavoidable ache in the grain of healing,
trying to boil the big words down to size — when a fox
lights out of hiding in the highway's grassy island
and arrows across the road before me, a rust-gold
flash from dark to dark. In that split second I catch
the compass-point of his nose, the quilled tip
of ears *in áirde*, the ruddering lift of a tail as he
streams by my sight, and I only have time
to lift my instinct's foot from the gas, clap hands, cry
'Fox!' in fright or invocation and he's gone, under
the metal fence, into the trees, home free. But all
the way home I hold him in my mind: a body
burning to its outer limits of bristle
with this moment, creature eyes alive with purpose, child
of time and impeccable timing
cometting across my vacant dark, a flow
of leaf-rust and foxy gold, risk-taker
shooting sure as a bird into the brush
with every hair in place, a splice
of apprehension, absolute, and pure indifference.
He is only getting on with his life, I know,
but engraved on my brain for good now

is his cave shape at full stretch, caught
in the brief blaze of my headlights
just like that . . . and still running.

Breaking Points

for Joe Butwin

They'll all want to break at some point,
if you can only find it, he says, hoisting
the wedgeheaded heavy axe and coming down with it
in one swift glittering arc: a single *chunnk*,
then the gleam of two half moons of maple
rolling over in the driveway. He finds
his proper rhythm, my strong friend from the west,
standing each half straight up,
then levelling swinging striking
dead centre: two quarters
fall apart from one another
and lie, off-white flesh shining,
on the cracked tarmac. I stand back
and watch him bend and bring to the chopping-place
a solid sawn-off wheel of the maple bough
the unexpected early snow brought down
in a clamorous rush of stricken leafage, a great weight
he walks gingerly under
and gently settles down.
                        When he tests it with his eye
I remember a builder of drystone walls
saying the same thing about rocks and big stones,
turning one over and over, hunting its line
of least resistance, then offering it a little
dull tap with his mallet: the stone, as if he'd
slipped the knot holding it together, opened
— cloned — and showed its bright unpolished
inner life to the world. Joe goes on logging
flat-out for an hour, laying around him
the split quarters, littering the tar-black driveway
with their matte vanilla glitter. Seeing
him lean on the axe-shaft
for a minute's headbent silence

in the thick of his handiwork,
                                    I remember
standing silent at the centre
of the living-room I was leaving for the last time
after ten years of marriage, the polished pine floor
scattered with the bits and pieces
I was in the aftermath taking with me,
the last battle still singing
in my head, the crossed limbs of the children
sofa-sprawled in sleep. And as soon
as he finishes and comes in, steam
sprouting from his red wet neck
and matted hair, dark maps of sweat
staining his navyblue T-shirt,
                                    I want to say
as he drains his second glass of lemonade
that this is the way it is
in the world we make and break
for ourselves: first the long green growing, then
the storm, the heavy axe, those shining remnants
that'll season for a year
before the fire gets them; this is the way
we flail our way to freedom of a sort,
and after the heat and blistering deed of it
how the heart beats in its birdcage of bone
and you're alone
with your own staggered body, its toll
taken, on the nervous verge of
exaltation. But I say nothing, just pour
more lemonade, open a beer, listen
to the tale he tells
of breakage back home — the rending-place
we reach when the labouring heart
fails us and we say,
What now? What else? What?

                                    And now
          in the dusk assembling outside the window
          I can see the big gouged maple
          radiant where the bough stormed off,
          and the split logs
          scattered and bright over the driveway — in what
          from this Babylonian distance looks like
          a pattern of solid purposes or the end of joy.

Walk, Night Falling, Memory of My Father

Downhill into town
between the flaring azaleas
of neighbour gardens: a cairn of fresh-cut logs
gives off a glow
of broken but transfigured flesh.

My father, meeting me years ago
off a train at Kingsbridge: greenish
tweed cap, tan gaberdine, leaning
on a rolled umbrella, the sun
in his eyes, the brown planes of his face
in shadow, and all of a sudden
old. The distance between us
closes to an awkward, stumbling,
short embrace. Little left

but bits and pieces: pints in Healy's
before tea; a drive with visitors
to the Sally Gap; my daughter making
game with his glasses; the transatlantic calls
for an anniversary, birthday,
or to the hospital
before his operations. Moments
during those last days
in the ward, under the big window
where the clouds over the golf course
would break or darken: his unexpected
rise to high spirits, my hand
helping his hand
hold the glass of water. And one memory
he kept coming back to,
of being a child in a white frock
watching his mother and another woman
in long white dresses and broad straw hats
recline in a rowing-boat on the Boyne

near Navan: how the boat rocked
side to side, the women smiling and
talking in low voices, and him
sitting by himself on the bank
in a pool of sunshine, his little feet
barely reaching the cool water. I remember
how the nurses swaddled his
thin legs in elastic bandages, keeping him
together for a day or two.

Uphill again, the dark now down
and the night voices
at their prayers and panicky conjurations,
one thrush still bravely
shaping in song
the air around him. Fireflies
wink on and off
in lovers' Morse, my own head
floating among them, seeing —
as each opens its heart in silence
and in silence closes —
just how large the dark is. Now,
cold moonglow casts
across this shaking summer world
a thin translucent skin
of snow; tall tree shapes
thicken, whispering; and on ghostly wings
white moths brush by. Indoors again,
I watch them — fallen angels
the size and shade of communion wafers —
beat dusted wings against the screen,
flinging themselves
at this impossible light.

Breakfast Room

1

The words have always stirred a sudden
surge of light, an air of new beginnings, something
neat and simple, a space
both elemental and domestic – because, perhaps
they bear a sort of innocent sheen
of privilege, a room so set apart
for an event so ordinary, a glimmer of ritual
where mostly we know only broken facts, bits and pieces
stumbling numbly into one another. Here
is a murmur of voices, discretion's homely music
of spoons on saucers, the decent movements
people make around each other – eager
to let themselves become themselves again
after the night's uncertain journeys. Or it may be
the secret knowing smiles that lovers save, sitting
to face one another in their quaint conspiracy
of hope and saying, *Pass the milk, please,* but meaning
Nothing has ever pleased me more
than how your naked shoulders and the small of your back
lay on my spread hands; your earlobe, tongue, wide eyes
entering half-frightened mine in the dark.

2

And in Bonnard's *The Breakfast Room,* you'll see
the impeccable ordinary order he finds in things:
white, slate-blue, the tablecloth bears its own still life
of teapot, cream pitcher, sugarbowl,
china cup and scalloped saucer, the half glass of raspberry juice,
bread in yellow napkins, that heaped dish
of purple figs and a peach. And, as if
accidental by the French windows —

through which morning light
passes its binding declarative sentence
on every detail – a woman stands
almost out of the picture, her back
against the patterned drapes, dressed to go out
and giving a last look back, her eyes and strict lips
asking directly, *You think this
changes anything?* Yet she too
is part of this stillness, this sense
that things are about to achieve
illumination. Beyond the window
a stone balustrade, and beyond that
nature's bluegreen tangle tangles
with the light that's melting one thing
into another – blue, scrubbed green, strawgold,
a house with a white and lilac roof
at the end of a sunstreaked avenue
on which the summer trees
are blobs of turquoise. Inside, quite distinct,
that woman is held to her last look back,
her sudden pulsebeat shaking
all the orderly arrangements
of the table. Through its
ambivalence of light, its double tongue
of detail and the world at large,
we are brought into the picture, into a kingdom
we might find under our noses: morning's
nourishment and necessary peace; a pause
on the brink of something always
edging into shape, about to happen.

Kitchen Vision

Here in the kitchen, making breakfast,
I find my own view of things
come to light at last: I loom, huge
freckled hands, in the electric kettle's
aluminum belly. In there

the limegreen fridge, military files
of spice jars, and that transfigured window
where the sun breaks flagrant in,
must all recede, draw off, and join
the tiny mourning face
of Botticelli's Venus, hung
above a Lilliputian door. In there

all our household effects
are strictly diminished, pared down
to brilliant miniatures
of themselves — the daily
ineluctable clutter of our lives
contained, clarified, fixed in place
and luminous in ordinary light,
as if seen once and for all
by Jan Steen or Vermeer. And off

in the silver distance, the baby
stares at me from her high chair
of a minute's silence,
and you — a mile away at the stove
turning the eggs — turn round

to look at me gazing
at my own
sharply seen misshapen self

in the kettle
that's just starting to sing,
its hot breath steaming.

Woman at Lit Window

Perhaps if she stood for an hour like that
and I could stand to stand in the dark
just looking, I might get it right, every
fine line in place: the veins of the hand
reaching up to the blind-cord, etch
of the neck in profile, the white
and violet shell of the ear
in its whorl of light, that neatly
circled strain against a black
cotton sweater. For a few seconds

she is staring through me
where I stand wondering what I'll do
if she starts on that stage of light
taking off her clothes. But she only
frowns out at nothing or herself
in the glass, and I think I could,
if we stood for an hour like this,
get some of the real details down. But
already, even as she lowers the blind,
she's turning away, leaving a blank

ivory square of brightness
to float alone in the dark, the faint
grey outline of the house
around it. Newly risen, a half moon
casts my shadow on the path
glazed with grainy radiance

as I make my slow way back
to my own place
among the trees, a host of fireflies
in fragrant silence and native ease
pricking the dark around me
with their pulse, ungovernable, of light.

Touch

In the corner, under a nightlight,
you sit in the rocking-chair
feeding the baby. From my pillow
I see the shadow-shapes
the two of you knit together,
how the line of your neck and throat
vanishes into the sweep of your hair
shawling the small bald crown of her head
that's pressed against
one full breast. Your hands
catch light, moulding the globe of shadow
her head composes, steadying
that wool-bundled body
to your flesh. Wherever I look
in that world of light and shade,
the two of you are touching
one another, leaving me
feeling exiled, not unhappy.
And she's asleep, and I'm asleep
when you stretch
your warm length again beside me.

The Cave Painters

Holding only a handful of rushlight
they pressed deeper into the dark, at a crouch
until the great rock chamber
flowered around them and they stood
in an enormous womb of
flickering light and darklight, a place
to make a start. Raised hands cast flapping shadows
over the sleeker shapes of radiance.

They've left the world of weather and panic
behind them and gone on in, drawing the dark
in their wake, pushing as one pulse
to the core of stone. The pigments mixed in big shells
are crushed ore, petals and pollens, berries
and the binding juices oozed
out of chosen barks. The beasts

begin to take shape from hands and feather-tufts
(soaked in ochre, manganese, madder, mallow white)
stroking the live rock, letting slopes and contours
mould those forms from chance, coaxing
rigid dips and folds and bulges
to lend themselves to necks, bellies, swelling haunches,
a forehead or a twist of horn, tails and manes
curling to a crazy gallop.

Intent and human, they attach
the mineral, vegetable, animal
realms to themselves, inscribing
the one unbroken line
everything depends on, from that
impenetrable centre
to the outer intangibles of light and air, even
the speed of the horse, the bison's fear, the arc
of gentleness that this big-bellied cow

arches over its spindling calf, or the lancing
dance of death that
bristles out of the buck's
struck flank. On this one line they leave
a beak-headed human figure of sticks
and one small chalky, human hand.

We'll never know if they worked in silence
like people praying — the way our monks
illuminated their own dark ages
in cross-hatched rocky cloisters,
where they contrived a binding
labyrinth of lit affinities
to spell out in nature's lace and fable
their mindful, blinding sixth sense
of a god of shadows — or whether (like birds
tracing their great bloodlines over the globe)
they kept a constant gossip up
of praise, encouragement, complaint.

It doesn't matter: we know
they went with guttering rushlight
into the dark; came to terms
with the given world; must have had —
as their hands moved steadily
by spiderlight — one desire
we'd recognise: they would — before going on
beyond this border zone, this nowhere
that is now here — leave something
upright and bright behind them in the dark.

Cows

They lay great heads on the green bank
and gently nudge the barbed wire aside
to get at the sweet untrodden grass, ears
at an angle flicking and swivelling. Something
Roman in the curled brow, massive
bony scaffolding of the forehead,
the patient, wary look that's
concentrated but detached, as if
the limits of being didn't matter
behind such a lumbering surge of things
in the flesh. Yet in their eyes some deep
unspeakable secret grudge — in part
perhaps their perfect knowledge
of the weight of the world
we hold them to. And something Dutch
about that recumbent mass, their couchant
hefty press of rumination, the solid globe
folded round the ribs' curved hull, barrelling
that enormous belly. The close
rich cud-smell where they stood
grinding down grass to milk
to mother us all; or the childhood stink of stalls
all milk and piss and dungy straw: all
that umbered word, *cowshed*, conjures.

I remember an Indian file of cows in mist
moving along the lake's lapped margin,
a black and white frieze against the green hill
that leaned over them: the sound
of their cloven steps in shallow water
reached me like the beat of a settled music
in the world we share, and they could have been
plodding towards Lascaux or
across broad prairie-seas of green, even
trampling water-edges such as this one —

trudging through the kingdom-come
of sagas and cattle-raids. Heads bent,
they stepped into mist and silence, the pooling
splash of their hooves a steady progress
that seemed to go on forever, forged
for an eternal trek to grass.

I love the way a torn tuft
of grassblades, stringy buttercup and succulent clover
sway-dangles towards a cow's mouth, the mild teeth
taking it in — purple flowers, green stems and yellow petals
lingering on those hinged lips
foamed with spittle. And the slow chewing sound
as transformation starts: the pulping roughness
of it, its calm deliberate solicitude, its own
entranced herbivorous pacific grace,
the carpet-sweeping sound of breath
huffing out of pink nostrils. Their eyelashes —
black, brown, beige, or white as chalk —
have a minuscule precision, and in the pathos
of their diminutive necessity
are the most oddly human thing about them:
involuntary, they open, close, dealing
as our own do
with what inhabits, encumbering,
the seething waves and quick invisible wilderness
of air, showing the one world
we breathe in
and the common ground — unsteady
under the big whimsical hum of weather —
we all walk across
one step at a time, and stand on.

Sea Dog

The sea has scrubbed him clean
as a deal table.
Picked over, plucked hairless,
drawn tight as a drum —
an envelope of tallow
jutting with rib cage, hips,
assorted bones. The once
precise pads of his feet
are buttons of bleached wood
in a ring of stubble. The skull —
bonnetted, gap-toothed, tapering
trimly to a caul of wrinkles —
wears an air
faintly human, almost ancestral.

Now the tide falls back
in whispers, leaving the two of us
alone a moment together. Trying
to take in what I see, I see
the lye-bright parchment skin
scabbed black by a rack of flies
that rise up, a humming chorus,
at my approach, settle again
when I stop to stare. These
must be the finishing touch, I think,
till I see round the naked neckbone
a tightly knotted
twist of rope, a frayed noose
that hung him up or held him under
till the snapping and jerking stopped.
Such a neat knot: someone
knelt safely down to do it,
pushing those soft ears back
with familiar fingers. The drag end

now a seaweed tangle around legs
stretched against their last leash.

And nothing more
to this sad sack
of bones, these poor enduring remains
in their own body bag. Nothing more.
Death's head here
holds its own peace
beyond the racket-world of feel and fragrance
where the live dog bent, throbbing
with habit, and the quick children
now shriek by on sand — staring,
averting. I go in over my head

in stillness, and see
behind the body and the barefoot children
how on the bent horizon to the west
a sudden flowering shaft of sunlight
picks out four pale haycocks
saddled in sackcloth
and makes of them a flared quartet
of gospel horses — rearing up,
heading for us.

Two Gathering

After supper, the sun sinking fast, Kate and I
have come to the shore at Derryinver
to gather mussels. Across cropped grass, rocks,
we walk to the water's edge where low tide
has exposed a cobbling of cobalt blue shells, others
tucked in clusters under a slick fringe
of seaweed. In my wellingtons
I enter shallow water, bending over
and wresting from their native perch
the muddy clumps of molluscs, rinsing them
in salt water that clouds and quickly clears again
as the tide laps, a slow cat, against me, then
pushing my handfuls into the white plastic bag
I've laid out of the water's way on seaweed.
Kate, in sneakers, is gathering hers
off dry rocks behind me: almost sixteen,
her slim form blossoms in jeans
and a black T-shirt, long hair falling over
as she bends, tugs, straightens
with brimming hands, leans like a dancer
to her white bag, looks out to me and calls
So many! Have you ever seen so many! her voice
a sudden surprise in that wide silence
we stand in, rejoicing — as she always does
and now I must — at the breathless plenitude
of the world, this wondrous abundance
offering itself up to us as if we were
masters of the garden, parts of the plenary
sphere and circle, our bodies belonging
to the earth, the air, the water, fellow creatures
to the secret creatures we gather
and will tomorrow kill for our dinner.
When I bend again — my hands pale groping starfish
under water — it is Kate's own life I fumble for,
from the crickets singing her name

the September afternoon she was born
to the balance she strikes
between separated parents, her passion
for maths, the names of her lost boys,
or the way she takes my arm
when we take a walk on Wing Road
or up the hill from Tully to the cottage. This instant
I can feel her eyes on my bent back, seeing me
standing over my ankles in water, the slow tide
climbing my boots, my cautious
inelastic stepping between elements
when I place the mussels I've gathered
in the bag. And if I turn to look,
I'll see a young woman rising out of sea-rocks, bearing
the salmon and silver air on her shoulders,
her two hands spilling a darkblue arc, about
to take a dancer's step: I hear the muffled clack
of live shells filling her bag.

In our common silence we stay
aware of one another, working together,
until she calls out — *Have you seen
their colours? Brown and olive and bright green
and black. I thought they were only navy blue* —
delighted by variety, the minute ripple of things
under water or changing in air, the quick patterns,
as if the world were one intricate vast equation
and she relished picking it over, seeing the figures
unfold and in a split surprising second
edge out of muddle into elegant sense, the way
she's explained to me her love of maths
as a journey through multiple views to a moment
of — she said it — 'vision', you simply see it
all in place before your eyes: a flowering branch
of impeccable sense, number and grace

shimmering in a single figure, a shard of truth
shining like the head of a new nail
you've just, with one stroke, driven home.

Feeling the drag and push of water, I know it's time
to move and I do, inching backwards, my hands
still scrabbling under rubbery weed fronds
for the mussels' oval stony bulk, their brief
umbilical resistance as I twist them
from their rock, swirl in water, add them
with drippling chill hands to the bag, sensing
the summer dusk falling all over us. *Dad, look! A heron!*
standing not twenty yards away from us
on the hem of the tide: a grey stillness
staring at nothing
then flicking his serpent-neck and beak
into the water and out, taking a single deliberate step
and then on slow opening wings
rising and flap-gliding across the inlet, inland, heavy
and graceful on the air, his legs
like bright afterthoughts dangling. *He's so big,*
she calls, *How does he do it?* and across
the raw distance of rock and water I call back,
It's the span of his wings, he uses the air,
thinking about question and answer, the ways
we're responsible to one another, how
we use our airy words to lift us up
above the dragging elements we live in
towards an understanding eloquent and silent
as blood is or the allergies I've handed
to her system — our bodies' common repugnance
to penicillin, sulfa — all the buried codes
that bind us in a knot even time
cannot untangle, diminishing, in a way,
the distance between us. *Did you see*, I hear my voice,

his legs? The way they dangled? Thin —
her voice comes back to me — *as sticks,*
and the colour of pearl. Funny
how he tucked them in, putting them away,
and she drops a castanet handful
of mussels into her bag.
                         My hands
are blueish, a small breeze riffles water,
the spur of land we're on
is drowned in shade: we've gathered enough
and it's time to go. She watches me wading
through bright, light-saving pools, reaches
a helping hand when I clamber up rock
above the seaweed line where she stands waiting
on grass the sheep have bitten to a scut,
their tidy shit-piles of black pellets
scattered all over. With pleasure we behold
the two bulging bags I've draped
in glistering layers of olivebrown bladderwrack,
both of us thinking of the dinner we'll have
tomorrow: brown bread, white wine, a green
salad, the steaming heaps of open shellfish
— ribboned in onion, carbuncled
with chunks of garlic — the plump dull-orange
crescent of each one gleaming
in its mottled shell, sea-fragrance curling off
the greybright salty peppered soup
they've offered up to us, and in it the brilliance
of lemon wedges swimming. At least once each summer
we have a family feast like this, and I picture
her delight in dipping buttered bread, laying
a hot mussel on her tongue, the squirt of sea-tang and flesh
against her teeth, sipping the wine that's still
a stranger to her palate, remembering
the way the sun went down behind the two of us

as we gathered dinner, as if our lives
were always together and this simple.
                                        Now
we stand side by side for a minute or two
in silence, taking the small bay in and the great shade
spreading over sea and land: across the water,
on a sloping headland of green fields, we see
how a stopped hand of sunlight still
in the middle distance lingers, brightening
one brief patch of ground with uncanny light
so I cannot tell if I'm looking at a moment past
of perfect knowledge, or a bright future
throbbing with promise. Then Kate
is giving me, again, her words: *I wonder
will it strike us over here*, is what
I hear her say — her words, unanswered,
hanging between us as we turn to go.

Blood

Two white horses in a field up the road:
a mare and her colt gleaming
out of the clouded day, at grass
in a windless wide silence,
the tenderness between them palpable
as that mild and serious something
in an empty chapel. The young one
is lying down, while his mother
browses a close circle round him,
but when she stops to stare at
the sound my footsteps make
on the road beyond the hedge
at the edge of their world,
the little one rises too and stands
looking, his two coal-black eyes
lingering on my strange shape, letting
out of his lustrous ebony muzzle
a faint, plaintive, interrogative
whickering.
        I know they're abroad
in every weather — wind snapping
at all corners of the valley, rain-squalls
making ditches roar, sunshine
cooking the air in clover — and it is for them
only weather, to be taken
with the same dense patience
they proffer to whatever happens, although
at intervals under a heavy shower,
after they've been standing as still
as creatures carved in quartz,
the mare will suddenly toss and gallop
round the fuchsia-bush and barbed-wire
border of the field, her colt
quickly following, his new legs
slow and a little stiff at first, but then,

with a springy, kicking bound
and a careless, elegant animation
of everything that makes the body
and the body move, he'll cut
to a perfect dash, tuck tight
to a tandem gallop, doubling his mother
on the run — picking up as he goes
whatever he knows from her,
but first how to warm the blood
she's given him, and then
how to be, increasingly, in the world.

Outing

Granted the Atlantic between us, I can only imagine
walking in on you asleep in an armchair
the nurses have pillowed, your white-haired head
and the powdery skin of your face tilted sideways,
your chin sinking into the sag of your breast
where one button in the pale blue frock's undone.

When you fell down that Sunday last summer
and your poor shoulder buckled under you,
I could tell — trying to lift that terrible weight
from the lavatory's slippery stone floor —
the way things were. Still, as every other summer,
you loved our drives out of Bloomfield
to the sea, loved sitting in the car up Vico Road,
staring off over water towards Howth or Bray,
Greystones, the Sugarloaf (as plain on a good day,
you'd say, as your hand). And no matter
even if it rained, it was always a cleansing
breath of fresh air for you, a sort of tranquil
hovering above things, the known world
close enough to touch: blackberry bushes
and high-gabled houses; foxglove and bracken;
the hundred steep steps down to the sea.
I used to wonder if it ever crossed your mind
that the next life you firmly believed in
might be something like that — the same peace
of simply sitting, looking at whatever was there
and passing: older couples with their dogs,
salted children streeling from the sea,
a parish priest swinging his black umbrella,
the occasional brace of lovers in step. Over
the lowered window you'd smile
your genteel *Good afternoon!* to them all,
and seem for this little while at least

almost out of reach of your old age — its slumped
and buzzing vacancies, blank panic, garbled talk.

But now, near another summer, they tell me
your temperature flares, falls, flares again,
and nothing to be done. Alive, they say,
but in ways not there at all, you've left us
and gone on somewhere, and I remember
how as kids we trailed your solid figure
when you pushed the youngest in his pram
and turned to call us all to catch up, *Hold on
to the pram now, don't let go.* I remember
the pounding silence when you'd hide
and all of a sudden come dashing out
behind your voice — your arms like wings,
laughing our names to the air around us,
the sound of your glad breath bearing down.
But when I appear in a week or so, I'm told
you won't know me, the way you mostly
don't know the others, and I remember
your phrase when I'd come home at last
after months at school: *I wouldn't know you,*
you'd say, holding me away at arm's length
or in a hug, *I just wouldn't know you,*
only this time the same delighted words
will die in your mouth, and you'll be
two puzzled milk-pale hazel eyes
staring at this bearded stranger. You've left
already, knowing well what I've no words for:
the smudge and shaken blur of things, bodies
floating by like clouds, brittle sunshine
flapping through a window to your lap,
days in their nameless, muffled procession
or the frank night-scurry of dream after dream,
each with its seepage, bat-flash, dear faces.

Here among woods and hills of New Hampshire
it's you I think of when I watch the mountains
appear and disappear in mist, the shape of things
changing by the minute. Were you with me now,
I'd show you these blowsy irises, and those
exploding globes of rhododendron, lady slippers
in the shade, or flagrant and shortlived the blaze
of the yellow day-lilies. You could listen out
for the pure soul music the hermit thrush makes
alone in the echo-chamber of the trees, his song
a blessing, you'd say, to your one good ear.
Side by side, we'd sit in this screened gazebo
facing Mount Monadnock, and you might try
the mountain's name a few times on your tongue,
getting it wrong, wrong again, until
you'd give your helpless laugh, give up, and say
For God's sake don't annoy me, will you,
whatever you call it. Can't I just call it
Killiney, Sugarloaf, or Howth — what matter?
We'd agree on this, *God knows*, and you
would sit back to enjoy the view, the delicious
sense of yourself just sitting — the way
we've always done, we're used to — pleased
for the moment with what we've got,
and pleased at how that big green hill
swims in and out of view as the mist
lifts and settles, and lifts, and settles.

Night Figure

She hovers over the ache of thresholds: that brass
doorknob and the cream paint chipped at the jamb
enter her face again, so close she doesn't notice.

She needs to hear us breathing, the three of us
pitching into sleep in the one room, tucked in
by a faint smell of face powder, sticky touch of lips.

Snare-beat of rain on the roof, the rain spitting
against the window. *It's spilling rain,*
she'll say to herself, *he'll be drowned out in it.*

As if underwater, she stands listening
to the house and all its stunned tongues
gather round her heart. Rumours of being

rush into the instant: a bus coughs by
on Clareville Road, quick steps
syncopate through rain, a bicycle bell

jings in the dark; *squeek squeek* of pedals
against wind and hill. When she moves
into their front bedroom, she sees

from the window a hurrying figure, hears
the little brickish *clik* that high heels
make on stone. A deep pain starts

to open her heart, and she's the secret
goings-on in hives — a slow gathering
and translation, the finished, overflowing

golden comb. Nothing now, *nothing* —
till his key comes fumbling the hall-door,
that sudden rush of air

as the door shuffles open, raw
against the hall's linoleum. A hint of stagger
in the hallway; heavy sit in the muffled chair

as his lidded eyes haze over, blinking: two hearts
heaving like mad. Behind closed doors
the air listens to a huffle of voices. She can feel,

when the petals of pain and rage
have closed again, her vacant relief. The house
complete at last: she can sleep. So

she lies beside his breath, her eyes open
and our house a hive of silence
around her head, her splitting head. Fingernails of rain

tapping for help against the window: *Let us in,
let us in, can't you?* Then thickened silence
levels the dark, taking the bed

she lies on, and she slides — nothing stops her —
into the wooden dusk
of wardrobes, down the sheer drop of sleep.

Heirloom

Among some small objects
I've taken from my mother's house
is this heavy, hand-size, cut-glass saltcellar:
its facets find her at the dining-room table
reaching for the salt or passing it to my father
at the far end, his back to the window.

The table's a timebomb: father hidden
behind the newspaper, mother filling our
plates with food; how they couldn't meet
each other's eyes. When he'd leave early
for an armchair, *Just a glance at the evening paper,*
she'd sit until — all small talk exhausted —

we kids would clear the tea-things away,
stack dirty dishes by the scullery sink,
and store the saltcellar in the press
where it would absorb small tears of air
till the next time we'd need its
necessary, bitter addition. Now it figures

on our kitchen table in Poughkeepsie,
is carried to the dining-room for meals —
its cheap cut glass outlasting flesh and blood
as heirlooms do. I take its salt
to the tip of my tongue, testing its savour,
and spill by chance

a tiny white hieroglyph of grains
which I pinch
in my mother's superstitious fingers
and quick-scatter over my left shoulder,
keeping at bay and safe
the darker shades.

Stone Flight

A piece of broken stone, granular granite, a constellation
of mica through its grey sky, one chalky pink band
splitting slabs of grey, it fits snug enough in the palm
of your hand. Toss it up and it falls, an arc saying *Yes*
to gravity again, and saying in its one dunt of a word
when it falls with a thump on the soft path, *I'm here
to stay*. At a pinch, you might strip things down to this:
compact and heavy the pressure on your hand; the light arc
as if things weighed nothing, casting off; the apogee
and turn, catching a different kind of light; the steady,
at the speed of gravity, descent; and then that dull but
satisfying *thunk* to stop, its cluster of consonantal solids
allowing no air in, no qualifying second thought
as it lands like the one kiss to his scratchy cheek
at greeting or bedtime you'd give your father, or maybe
rolls an inch or two — depending on the chance of grit,
pebbles, the tilt of ground at this precise point
in the wide world, or the angle of itself it falls on. Not,
however, that *grunt* the condemned man makes
some fifty far-fetched seconds or so
after the injection has done our dirty work, the slump
of his head and just once that grunt as the body
realises its full stop, almost surprised. Nor yet the small
grunt of surprised satisfaction you've heard
when you're as deep inside and around one another
as you two can be, body bearing body away and
you push, once, and flesh grunts with a right effort
that seems outside, beyond the two of you, something
old and liberated, a sort of joyous punctuation point
in the ravelling sentence that leaves you both as one
breathless wrap of skin and bone, your double weight
hardly anything as you kiss your way down and back
to your own selves, maybe rolling an inch or two
and then lie still, alive, in matter again, the tick of it
starting to fill the silence. But not that either — just a stone

that leaves your opened hand, lets go of you, ascends
to its proper pitch this once and descending, kissing
gravity every inch, to hit the ground you picked it from
with hardly a thought, and staying there, mica stars
glittering in its granite firmament, a stone among stones
in the dust at a verge of meadowgrass and wild carrot.

Bat

With no warning
and only the slightest
whisshing sound
it was in the room with me,
trapped and flashing
wall to wall. Flat
black leather wings
that never stop, body
become a baby fist,
tiny head
blindly peering,
a wild heart
out of its element.

Between its teeth
it needles a piercing
inaudible pulse-scream
that sets its course
and keeps it beating,
barely grazing
walls, wardrobe,
chest of drawers, all
— pitch pine, walnut,
Irish oak — smelling
of outdoors, I suppose,
and sending it
round the bend
while I
try to follow its
dodgy swerves, duck
when it flutters at me,
fumble after
with my eyes.

This all happens
in a fathomless
daylight silence
which binds us
for a hypnotised
little while,
making me feel
as the creature
circles and circles
that I've been kissed
repeatedly
in sleep, light lips
brushing, gone.

At last — by luck
as much as
navigation — it flits
through the window
I've scrambled open,
leaving me
to track its zigzags
over bright grass,
by light afflicted,
desperate
for the dark. Now,

months later,
I still remember
how it tackled exactly
its woeful task,
a heartbeat holding it
to scents and glimmers
of bloodsap, wingwhisper,
nightsqueaks, void,
the sheer (to my ear)

stoic silence
of the whole operation
showing rightly
the likes of us
how to behave
in a tight corner:

Keep quiet
keep moving
try everything
more than once
steer
by glancing touches
aftershocks
the fleeting grace
of dark advances
quick retreats
till you find
in your way
with no warning
the window
open.

Women Going

You know the ordinary ways they go
from you and from the stark daylight
staring through an open door. This girl
leans her lips to the beak of a dove
she holds against her heart as if
insinuating the best way out and back
and whispering, *Now I have to go.*

On a stone doorpost the young wife
arches her stopped body, one hand
flat across her belly, the other
raised to straighten the seamless veil
through which the full moons of her earrings
just appear, signalling a change of state
and no way back to the here and now
of things, to the honeysuckle open air
she's been breathing. This lady of the house

holds up one necklace after another
chosen from the jewelbox a servant offers
and eyes the way it might belong
between the jut of her neckbone
and where her breasts begin, fitting her
for the road that opens ahead now
and night falling: *This one*, she says
at last, picking the pearls with a clasp
curved like a wishbone. And now

across the busy street you see a man
lean into the back of a taxi
where a woman's face is barely visible
looking back into his and not flinching
as they dispossess each other into absence,
and the door in that black cloud closes over

whatever it is they say above the roar
of rush-hour traffic. He bends away,

and you know when he looks again
she'll be gone, and in her place will be
this absence beating its stone wings
over every ordinary corner of the day
she's left, and left him in.

Pause

The weird containing stillness of the neighbourhood
just before the school bus brings the neighbourhood kids
home in the middle of the cold afternoon: a moment
of pure waiting, anticipation, before the outbreak of anything,
when everything seems just, seems *justified*, just hanging
in the wings, about to happen, and in your mind you see
the flashing lights flare amber to scarlet, and your daughter
in her blue jacket and white-fringed sapphire hat
step gingerly down and out into our world again
and hurry through silence and snow-grass
as the bus door grinds shut
and her own front door flies open and she finds you
behind it, father-in-waiting, the stillness in bits
and the common world restored as you bend
to touch her, take her hat and coat from the floor
where she's dropped them, hear the live voice of her
filling every crack. In the pause
before all this happens, you know something
about the shape of the life you've chosen to live
between the silence of almost infinite possibility and that
explosion of things as they are — those vast unanswerable
intrusions of love and disaster, or just the casual scatter
of your child's winter clothes on the hall floor.

Ants

A black one drags the faded remains of a moth
backwards over pebbles, under blades of grass.
Frantic with invention, it is a seething gene
of stubborn order, its code containing no surrender,
only this solitary working frenzy that's got you
on your knees with wonder, peering into the sheer
impedimentary soul in things and into
the gimlet will that dredges the dead moth
to where their dwelling is, the sleepy
queen's fat heart like a jellied engine
throbbing at the heart of it, her infants
simmering towards the light. On your table
a tiny red one picks at a speck of something
and hurries away: one of its ancestors
walked all over the eyes of Antinous, tickled
Isaac's throat, or scuttled across the pulse
of Alcibiades, turning up at the Cross
with a taste for blood. In a blink, one enters
your buried mother's left nostril, brings a message
down to your father's spine and shiny clavicle,
or spins as if dizzy between your lover's
salt breasts, running its quick indifferent body
ragged over the hot tract of her, scrupulous
and obsessive into every pore. And here's one
in your hairbrush, nibbling at filaments
of lost hair, dandruff flakes, the very stuff
of your gradual dismantling. Soap, sugar, a pale
fleck of semen or the blood-drop from a mouse
the cat has carried in, it's all one grist to this mill
that makes from our minute leftovers
a tenacious state of curious arrangements — the males
used up in copulation, females in work, life itself
a blind contract between honeydew and carrion,

the whole tribe surviving in that complex gap
where horror and the neighbourly virtues, as we'd say,
adjust to one another, and without question.

Shed

You wouldn't know it had been there at all, ever,
the small woodshed by the side of the garage
that a falling storm-struck bough demolished
some seasons back, the space and remains now
overcome by weeds, chokecherry, wild rose brambles.
But, at the verge of where it stood, a peach tree
I'd never seen a sign of before has pushed
its skinny trunk and sparse-leaved branches up
above that clutter into the thoroughfare of light
and given us, this fall, a small basketful
of sweet fruit the raccoons love too and sit at midnight
savouring, spitting the stones down where the shed
used to stand — those bony seeds ringing along
the metal ghost of the roof, springing into the dark.

Unfinished

The house next door but one to this one
never happened, and all connected with its
shadow life are shadows now and maybe
tremble in the grassblades growing where
the planked earthen floor would have lain
between two walls facing east and west,
the front to where morning light still spills
over the bony shoulder of Diamond Hill,
the back taking in a flank of Tully Mountain
and the valley where the Atlantic evening
scatters its last handfuls. A half-built
shell of stone, it seems to stand as if
just broken from a dream, stunned,
its rags and tatters of raw stone
standing as a solitary gable, a single wall,
the big lintel-piece balanced almost on air,
the dead handyman having neatly slotted
stone to separate stone like the syntax
of a language that once trusted itself
and the sense it was making, left no gaps
of incoherence, nothing unsaid, knew
exactly how things fitted, could tell
the perfect place for any solid shape that
could be gathered from the field itself
into which it's lapsing now, a few
stones at a time, but mostly — in time
as we measure it — standing up to cows,
rough winds, persistent rain.
                                        I'm told
the man who began building left it as is
when the family of the wife he'd intended
denied permission. So he left and went
to America, they say, though no one knows
what happened to the woman. What
could her eyes have done, I wonder,

when she passed this way in the wake
of two cows, or going to Mass on Sunday?
I can't imagine the pause she'd make
on the far side of the sally bank, the drenched
fuchsia brushing her shawl, that gaping
half-made body looking blankly back at her,
and beyond it — through what would have been
their bedroom wall — the sheen of the lake
they'd have seen with some wonder
under a hundred lights. Somewhere
in Chicago or South Boston it may be
he tried a while to remember, or couldn't
help the hard walls his hands had put up
falling across his sleep, and then nothing.
                                         I know
the house I live in is — under its
whitewashed mortared skin — the same as his,
although it folded round itself, was finished,
and the weather that enters is a play of light
through glass, only the safe sounds of rain
on the roof or wind in the chimney. But I love
what he left, blunt masterpiece as it is
of understatement, its tight-lipped simplicity
getting the point across in its own terms
and caring for nothing but the facts
of the matter, the exact balance between
how this gesture registers in the world
and how the hard thing that happened, happened.

One Morning

Looking for distinctive stones, I found the dead otter
rotting by the tideline, and carried all day the scent of his
    savage
valediction. That headlong high sound the oystercatcher
    makes
came echoing through the rocky cove
where a cormorant was feeding and submarining in the bay
and a heron rose off a boulder where he'd been invisible,
drifted a little, stood again — a hieroglyph
or just longevity reflecting on itself
between the sky clouding over and the lightly ruffled water.

This was the morning after your dream of dying, of being
    held
and told it didn't matter. A butterfly went jinking over
the wave-silky stones, and where I turned
to go up the road again, a couple in a blue camper sat
smoking cigarettes over their breakfast coffee
and talking in quiet voices, first one then the other answering,
their radio telling the daily news behind them. It was warm.
All seemed at peace. I could feel the sun coming off the water.

Six O'Clock

Steamy mushroom weather. Under the white pines
a smell of turpentine and dust. A young woman
swings by, her handbag the colour of ten-year-old claret.

In the cemetery someone is playing a mouth-organ:
'There's No Place Like Home' rises on the surprised air
while light-leaved saplings nod eager affirmatives

to each other (*yes yes, that's it, exactly*), stop a minute
to take things in, then again to affirmation.
I can smell the one pinetree cut down this morning

and carted away, leaving only this white stump of a thing
and its glimmer of dust, the lingering scent of resin. Airborne,
a glitter-flock of starlings expands, contracts, expands

like a beating brain, a heart pulsing, its every element
answerable. Our cat sees with her ears, each swivelling
to catch the drift of things on the breeze, as I go on

naming one thing at a time (*orchard, silo, hawk, eyelid,
sea-mark, bloody cranesbill, slate*), making windows
to peer into . . . exactly what? The hour that's in it?

In Late February

As when the siege of some great city lifts

and they sit outside on steps drinking hot tea
and making mindless chatter, I hear my daughter
after two months of snow and a sudden thaw —
feeling sun heat the hair at the back of her neck —
say the word *grass* over and over, seeing a strip
of pale green the robins are already mining.

Driving to work last Sunday, I thought the soul
might be a handful of blown snow, its scattered
shattered light vanishing before my eyes.
And yesterday, from a maple branch, I could taste
the barest trace of sweetness, encased
in a blade of ice where the branch had fractured.

Every night now, under the blazing stars
and over the ice cracking like toffee brittle,
a dog barks all night like my mind, keeping
the entire neighbourhood awake. But when
I meet the barefoot boy in the coloured waistcoat
walking home past midnight in a cloud of song

I know the old season is almost over,
and I almost love my own shadow again —
its attached levity making light of obstacles
and accelerating over known ground
like a catbird lost in the deep leaves of summer
but for its persistent *pursue-me!* music.

Weather

After three or four days of persistent rain
something like panic sets in, a sense
of being smothered by wet noise,
nowhere to turn and nothing to be done
but hang on, hold out until some fresh
thing happens. I think of middle age like this,
when you can see bleakness
and no change, farther outlook only
more of the same, and you find yourself
saying this is the way things have to be
for good now. Even those you love
get stranger and stranger: you grow
more fragile with each other, thinking
of warm things in their burrows
who listen to the wind's loud mouth at the door —
how it bites and gouges all above ground.

But then the weather settles abruptly,
sudden as a reprieve, and that's the way
you could start to see your life — as if you'd
been let off again and not discovered
wanting. In the suddenly auspicious
light-breaking breezes out of the southeast
the sturdy panels of a well-made shirt —
white cotton drying on the line — seems
a hopeful canvas on which, between
now and evening, anything
can happen, wind filling the shirt-sail
with a fresh taste for adventure,
and even after eleven at night you can see
the pair of swans on the lake are two
incandescent glimmers of possibility
under a fitful moon, while the last
blackbird won't give in to the dark
but goes on, invisible as he is, singing

until your daughter wakes and says,
Dad, I can hear the bird, it's laughing.
Is the rain all gone? And before
you can tell her how things are, she is
asleep again, and the house is spinning
its own sure silence round your lives.

from *Martha's Vineyard in October*

Noisy all morning under downpouring rain
are the upper stories of scrub oak and beech
and the bluejay with beaked acorn who stands
screeching on a rain-glazed porch railing
when the clouds thin and sunshine starts to stiffen,
making a breakthrough. They wake, rise and
move around each other, organise their lives for
a few days away: two families, grandparents, friends,
they mind the children, sit down to breakfast
with wet hair, three generations circling in surprise
to find themselves like this, intimate strangers.

❖

In the poison-olive tree a cardinal snags a berry
and squinnies through the rain and glow of everything.
They see things in their hungers making do, and hear
the kids swapping curiosities: was that a whale
they saw, sudden island of dark on the bright sea,
breaching and disappearing and not coming back
no matter how long they stay peering out
over the tree-tops through the rain, seeing nothing,
yet still thinking, *How well off we are*
here in this high sea-girt place facing south
towards shoals of light, invisible the next landfall.

❖

The sun, on burnished wings, sweeps into the bedroom
and lights up half her face where she lies reading
a mystery, wondering how it will turn out.
When he sits down beside her, she raises her arms
to take him in, drawing his face to hers, his mind
lagging a bit aside from them and floating out
to where the waves glitter a persistent forced march

south towards the open sea, over which this morning
two dark arrows of geese went barking, that sound
bringing them to themselves from sleep, and covering
the true bed music they made as their bodies
became a small boat they tried to steady, staying here.

❖

When brightness breaks up the rain, the place
swims in what they all feel but cannot call
blessedness, and before they start to speak again
they know, and are content to know, just the air
standing in a sphere of light, an embrace of airlight
taking all things to itself — trees, green openings of grass,
grey clapboard walls and gables, the biting colours
of chrysanthemums in a crystal vase, and in the distance
white slow-motion explosions where unheard surf
dashes itself, draws back, and dashes itself against the land.
The moment past, they fall to talk again. What happened?

❖

Drowsing in sunshine, she's on the edge of enlightenment
again, she thinks, but only sleep comes down
with its dream of surf breaking on sand, the way
each slate wave buckles and lets the light out
in a rush, then restores itself to dark water. He's afraid
for her in the force of the sea, that battering at sand
where a dozen sanderlings do their mechanical tango
with the lickety-split fringe of ocean: this is their world, all
salt and uproar, and they make a comic thing of it, unlike
how these two hold each other in the riptide — feeling
the ground give way, that felt solid where they stood.

Stop

We slowed and pulled over beside the body
on a side-road in the valleyed shadow
of two blunt hills near Sligo. With its
digger's claws, dust-encrusted pelt, a darkened
curl of blood between bared teeth, the creature
lay as if asleep, flies on its eyelids, when I stopped
the engine and got out to see my first badger,
a solid black and white case of absence,
and you got out too, took one quick look,
then walked ahead to the clump of bushes
briaring over a high bank, and leaned in
among the brambles and began picking
the fat blackberries, till you had enough
to bring two handfuls and spill them
on the flat dashboard, where they glistened
onyx and veiny vermilion when we
took them one by one and put them
in each other's mouth, splitting
each plump-fleshed bitter-sweetness
between our teeth, tonguing and swallowing
the dark ripeness of it. We drove on then,
the green after-rain peace of that deep valley
holding us a half-hour more
till we found the main road and turned
north on it into the thundershower
that would wash the badger's blood
away from our stopping-place, but not
the memory of it, nor of love
fenced round by barbs and brambles
yet flourishing among the fruits of the earth
and filling her hands for me.

Bonnard, Daydreaming

Setting off without prologue or blessing,
you open the fish and put its bones on show:
somewhere between carmine and royal blue,
the flesh nestles between them.

Stone boats of Giza and Heliopolis
sunk in sand; the pyramids only teardrops
of stony light: you stand beside them
in your apricot frock, blocking each one out in turn.

Your shinbone makes the best music, hours
of the same song turning in my hand. Our daily life
is repeated over there: *Apricots, the whole tree
full of them . . . the dark leaves.* Over there

they hand out pomegranates, almonds, sweet figs,
cast a wooden flail after flocks of birds: their sky
is loaded with herons, moorhens, green pigeons
and what they call the laughing goose,

his black neck a shock on his white body. So
a comb matters over there, its tortoiseshell teeth
flashing in another light, and your hair matters,
and the curve of your back I've curled around,

and the cusp of tufted shadow that comes to light
when you bend over on the bathroom tiles,
the towel's white turban around your head
and under it the rest of you

smiling everywhere without a stitch on
here in the morning
before the world knocks, knocking us into
these whispers, pencil-thin, we live in.

Itinerary

Feel a passion for invisibility, be a fly on the wall,
the pitcher's ear, the child in the corner
with his eyes clenched. Like a dog going round
and round, you circle a space you've come back to,
trying to find some comfort, something that says
you're at home now. Pray for the enlarging hush
of the owl's ear, the hawk's high wide-angle lens
reading the world like a map. Your friend's
been weeding his potato drills. He stops and sits
on a rock for a cigarette. The sun has been shining
for days and days. *It's a gift*, he tells you.
A solitary thrush, with his heart in his mouth,
performs a dozen songs at dusk, none finished,
as if it were just himself and the world. Such
tense composure swells that speckled breast, warm
in late daylight: you see the beak open and close,
shivering into music. Wrapped in the spider's
winding-sheet, a bluebottle makes another music,
sawing the room in half: you note, till it stops,
each repeated live driving note. When you throw
open the door, the scent of fresh-cut grass swims in
and a huge yellow-edged summer moon hangs
alone in a powder-blue sky: a bright dense body
dependent on nothing. Stand back from nothing:
pussyfoot no more from the crux of the matter: you
must travel at the speed of light, not looking back.

Oasis

To enter this cool space
settles the stutter of nerves
that has taken your gaze
from the tall blue fall

of mountains in the distance:
you step into a ring of shade
in which you find this deep,
reflective, necessary source,

this simple joy
the committed body catches at
as if at the last gasp
of home: first the felt

luxury of shadow, its way
of slowing you down to know
what flesh is again, then
that sound the pool makes

stirring at its banks and
from the heart. *Water* . . .
You keep saying
its wedded syllables

as if they were enough,
their open and closing vowels
a cry before satisfaction,
though when you reach

its very self — the hard bright
splash of it — it's something
speechless, simply *known*,
the fluent pure give of it

first to the fever of your skin
and after
to that naive but greedy need
your tongue knows:

it fills, overspills
the heart in your mouth
like another life
gasping all its secrets at once,

and everything grows clear
as day breaking
through muslin curtains
to keep you here, where breath

swims in the saturated radiance
we came from, as if
two could go on saying
at the same time

the one good word.

Fenceposts

Inside each of these old fenceposts
fashioned from weathered boughs and salt-bleached
   branches
(knotholes, wormy ridges, shreds of bark still visible)
something pulses with a life that lies outside our language:
for all their varicose veins and dried grain lines,
these old-timers know how to stand up
to whatever weather swaggers off the Atlantic or over
the holy nose of Croagh Patrick, to ruffle
the supple grasses with no backbone — which seem
endlessly agreeable, like polite, forebearing men
in a bar of rowdies. Driven nails, spancels
of barbed wire, rust collars or iron braces — the fenceposts
tighten their hold on these and hang on, perfecting
their art and craft of saying next to nothing
while the rain keeps coming down, the chapping wind
whittles them, and the merciless sun
just stares and stares: yearly the shore is eaten away
and they'll dangle by a thread until salvaged
and planted again in the open field, which they bring
to an order of sorts, showing us how to be at home
and useful in adversity, and weather it.

Acknowledgements

The poems on pages 11 to 90 appear in the following books published first by The Gallery Press: *Wildly for Days* (1983), *What Light There Is* (1987), *As If It Matters* (1991) and *So It Goes* (1995). Most of these poems, and the more recent poems on pages 91 to 105, appear in *Relations: New and Selected Poems*, published in the United States (1998) by Graywolf Press.

The epigraph from 'Throughout Our Lands' translated by Czeslaw Milosz and Peter Dale Scott appears in *The Collected Poems 1931-1987* of Czeslaw Milosz, published by the Ecco Press, NY and Viking/Penguin, 1988.

Notes

page 28 The English explorer Henry Hudson thought he had found the chimeral Northwest Passage when he sailed up what is now the Hudson River. By the time he'd reached a point somewhat north of Poughkeepsie, he realised his mistake. The 'wet sea-boy' is borrowed from *Henry IV, Part Two* (III.i.27); in some texts it is 'sea-son'.

page 40 Chicago Hall is an academic building that houses the departments of foreign languages in Vassar College.

page 48 The italicised phrase is from John Donne's *Satire III* ('On a huge hill, / Cragged and steep, Truth stands, and hee that will / Reach her, about must, and about must goe').

page 65 Among the things in my head when I was writing this were Seamus Heaney's 'Bog' poems.

page 85 Most of these figures refer to pieces of sculpture in *The Greek Miracle: Classical Sculpture from the Dawn of Democracy*, at the Metropolitan Museum of Art, New York, 1993.

page 101 The italicised image is from 'Gathering Apricots' by Czeslaw Milosz, translated by the author and Robert Hass, in *Provinces*, the Ecco Press, NY, 1991.